Dear Parent:
Your child's love of reading starts here!

Every child learns to read in a different way and at his or her own speed. Some go back and forth between reading levels and read favorite books again and again. Others read through each level in order. You can help your young reader improve and become more confident by encouraging his or her own interests and abilities. From books your child reads with you to the first books he or she reads alone, there are I Can Read Books for every stage of reading:

SHARED READING
Basic language, word repetition, and whimsical illustrations, ideal for sharing with your emergent reader

BEGINNING READING
Short sentences, familiar words, and simple concepts for children eager to read on their own

READING WITH HELP
Engaging stories, longer sentences, and language play for developing readers

READING ALONE
Complex plots, challenging vocabulary, and high-interest topics for the independent reader

ADVANCED READING
Short paragraphs, chapters, and exciting themes for the perfect bridge to chapter books

I Can Read Books have introduced children to the joy of reading since 1957. Featuring award-winning authors and illustrators and a fabulous cast of beloved characters, I Can Read Books set the standard for beginning readers.

A lifetime of discovery begins with the magical words **"I Can Read!"**

Visit www.icanread.com for information
on enriching your child's reading experience.

Pinkalicious®
Story Time

by Victoria Kann

HARPER

An Imprint of HarperCollinsPublishers

We were at a book fair,

waiting in line.

I was going to meet my hero,

Princess Plum!

I have all of her books.

Meet the
Author of
the
Princess
Plum
books.

Princess Plum is kind.

She is smart.

She grants magic wishes

and wears a sparkly purple tiara.

I love her stories.

"I hope she signs my book,"
I told Mommy.

I couldn't believe I was going to meet
a real princess at last.

But when we got

to the front of the line,

I was very surprised.

Instead of a princess, I saw a man!

"Is Princess Plum a man?" I said.

"I'm Syd Silver." The man laughed.

"I'm the author of Princess Plum.

That means I write books about her."

"But how can you write about
being a magic princess
if you aren't one?" I asked.
"When you're an author,
you can tell all sorts of stories,"
said Mr. Silver.

"Princess Plum is a character
I made up.
Stories can be about anyone
or anything you want.
Just use your imagination!"

That afternoon,
I couldn't stop thinking
about what Mr. Silver had said.
I decided to give it a try.

I imagined I could fly

and wrote about soaring

around Pinkville.

In my story,

I made the clouds into cotton candy.

After that,

I wrote about a tea party

with dancing spoons and cups.

I wrote about a garden

growing under my bed.

I wrote about a family of pirates

that lives inside the washing machine.

I couldn't stop writing!

At dinnertime,

I wrote about a broccoli jungle

and sweet-potato mountains.

Broccoli jungle
Sweet-potato mountains

At bedtime,

I wrote about

a pair of bunny slippers

hopping all over the house.

At school on Monday,

I came up with more ideas.

I wrote them all down.

I was too busy to listen

to my teacher, Ms. Penny.

I was writing about a pink panda
when Ms. Penny tapped my shoulder.
"Pinkalicious," she said,
"what are you doing?"

I gulped.

I told Ms. Penny everything,

about meeting the author Syd Silver

and writing stories all day long.

"I'm sorry for not paying attention,"

I said.

"Well," said Ms. Penny,

"paying attention is very important.

But so is being creative.

I think I have an idea."

"Listen everybody," said Ms. Penny.

"This week,

you are all going to be authors!

We will have special writing time

so you can work on your stories.

And on Friday, we'll have

our own class book festival."

At recess, we talked about our ideas.

"I'm writing about a
penguin named Percy," said Molly.

"I'm writing about a family of giants
who live in the rain forest,"
said Rose.

Alison's book was the biggest surprise.

It didn't have any words!

She was making a comic-book story

with only pictures.

We worked hard all week.

I finished the story about flying

through the cotton-candy clouds.

I drew the cover and added
an "about the author" page.
"Pinkalicious is from Pinkville,"
I wrote.
"She loves writing, baking cupcakes,
and anything pink!"

On Friday,

we read our stories out loud.

We signed our books.

It was so much fun!

Before I went home,

I told Ms. Penny

I had one last thing to write.

Dear Mr. Silver,

You may not be a princess who grants wishes, but your books are full of magic. Thank you for helping me see that I am a writer too!

Pinkalicious